Wise Parent

The Essential Guide to Raising a Child

by

Dean Michaels

WISE PARENT
The Essential Guide to Raising a Child

Copyright © 2011 by Dean Michaels

WiseParentAuthor@gmail.com

Published by All Wisdom Media
Los Angeles, California

ISBN 978-1-929989-89-8

Library of Congress Control Number: 2011913845

First Printing: October 2011

Printed in the United States of America

To my parents,
with deep love and everlasting gratitude

Contents

Introduction

Parents and children benefit most from a parenting philosophy that is based on a comprehensive set of wise principles and practices. The word *wisdom* has always referred to the most valuable insights for living life well, for knowing what ought to be pursued in life and how best to do so. Wisdom represents knowledge that is tested and true; knowledge that—when applied—helps ensure highly desirable and worthy possibilities become a reality. Following the path of wise parenting results not only in more positive outcomes, but also in much less pain in the life of the child and the life of the parent.

Wise Parent lays out an approach that embraces all the essential aspects of childrearing. It emphasizes the wisdom, values, and skills a parent needs to learn, demonstrate, and pass on to their child, and the insights to make the parenting experience itself more effective and fulfilling. This incisive guidebook offers parents advice that is wide-ranging, highly clarifying, and deeply potent, in a format that is succinct enough to be reread from time to time so that it can achieve its maximum desired effect.

Raising a child makes a parent more experienced at raising children, but it does not necessarily make a parent all that wise! Although you will learn many things about life as you raise your child and will therefore acquire some wisdom in the process, your child will benefit most if you already have considerable wisdom to offer them. It is this important role *Wise Parent* can play, by imparting to you the vital teachings of parental wisdom—wisdom that has been gathered and distilled from countless sources old and new, wisdom that is at the very heart of truly successful parenting.

This book is much more than a collection of great parenting tips. Its comprehensive and balanced orientation—its integral orientation—synthesizes all the essential teachings into a meaningful whole that is instructive and inspirational. A parenting book that is infused with the spirit of both idealism and practicality can serve to pull you and your child in the direction of integral growth. You certainly cannot rely on popular culture with its many negative influences to help you accomplish such growth. Nor can you rely on educational institutions, which typically neglect to ennoble their students or turn them into mature and responsible adults. Only a parent who is committed to growing in wisdom, virtue, and skill is able to guide their child to thriving maturity. Only a well-informed, well-rounded parenting approach that draws upon the best timeless and timely principles can capably meet all the challenges of raising a child in the twenty-first century.

Wise Parent is a manual that covers the entire span of time during which a child is under the care of his or her parents. It is therefore useful for expecting parents, parents of young children, and parents of school-age children including teens. Each of its one hundred chapters is a powerful lesson on a key aspect of parenting; a lesson that conveys an indispensable truth a parent should know and follow. Because the lessons are not age-specific, whenever you read each lesson and reflect on it, determine how it could best be utilized in your own parenting experience given your child's present stage of development.

I am confident you will soon come to regard *Wise Parent* as a trusted companion and an invaluable guide on the long journey of raising your child. You will also realize that it is as much a book of self-improvement for the parent as it is a book of lessons to impart to the child. So reread this book often, use it as a checklist to make sure you are addressing all of your parenting responsibilities, and recommit yourself to the task of growing both as a parent and as a person.

As you absorb and apply these principles and practices of wise parenting, the insights they reveal will in time resound as your own inner voice of guiding wisdom. You will be grateful for having been richly rewarded, and you will take pleasure and pride in a child who is well on their way to living a healthy, happy, fruitful, and meaningful life—a wisdom-based life.

1.

Your Children Are Your Biggest Impact on the World

Unless you happen to touch the lives of many people through your work, your biggest long-term impact on the world will be through your children. As you help shape your children, they will in turn help shape all those with whom they come in contact, including the family they may start one day and its countless offspring. Realize how consequential childrearing is, but don't let this realization dishearten you or dissuade you from having more children. Allow it instead to increase your commitment to performing your parenting duties with ever-growing knowledge, skill, and dedication.

Embrace the fact that parenting—like life itself—is neither constant fun nor constant struggle, but rather a natural, maturing, demanding, humbling, joyful, wondrous, and rewarding journey that leaves indelible marks on yourself, your child, and the world.

2.

There Is No Magic Formula for Becoming a Great Parent and Raising Great Children

There is no simple winning approach to raising great children, nor is there one right answer to most parenting challenges. Therefore, do not be concerned that you may never become a perfect parent or your child a perfect child. Every human being, regardless of age, is by nature unique, complex, and evolving—learning from mistakes and seeking the way forward. How could there be a precise formula for ensuring that this process always runs smoothly or that it reaches a definitive goal?

Don't obsess about your parenting abilities or about providing *everything* for your child, or even about following all of the one hundred principles and practices of wise parenting without fail. Simply be glad that there is much you *can* do to be a good parent and to raise good children, and apply yourself earnestly to this task.

3.

An Authoritarian and Overcontrolling Method of Parenting Is Harmful

In fulfilling your duty of becoming a good parent and raising good children, do not adopt an authoritarian style of parenting. Don't demand constant obedience from your child or emphasize discipline above all else. Don't be aggressive in your manner or demeanor or threaten your child often or sternly. That kind of behavior results in a hostile atmosphere at home. If you try to force anything on your child too much, not only will your child rebel now, but also later as a young adult. If you seek total control over every aspect of your child's life and nature, not only will your efforts prove futile, but your anger and frustration at your failed attempts may lead you to overreact frequently, which you will later regret and your child may forever resent.

A desire for exerting excessive control often stems from wrong motivations on your part— considerations of what suits *your* needs or what is good *in general*, rather than what is good for this child at this particular stage of their development.

Instead of wanting complete control over your child as you would of property that you own, see yourself as a good steward who has been entrusted to properly nurture a precious child.

4.

A Hands-Off Style of Parenting Is Irresponsible

If an overcontrolling method of parenting is at one extreme, the hands-off approach to raising children is at the other. It is true that your child will continue to grow even if they are provided with only the basic necessities—just as a plant would. But don't confuse physical growth, which happens quite naturally and easily, with proper and healthy maturing. It is not enough to provide your child with love and acceptance and otherwise leave them with little constructive guidance, supervision, or discipline. As innocent as children may be, they do not come prepackaged with only good tendencies. They are also not above developing bad habits, nor are they beyond associating with bad company. If you mistakenly believe that this is the case, you will not place sufficient emphasis on the need to develop your child's good character and good judgment.

Never assume that your child's maturing process will necessarily work out successfully of its own accord. At best, this is wishful thinking or mere gambling; at worst, nonchalant laziness or parental neglectfulness. Recognize, therefore, that the only time to apply the largely hands-off style of parenting is when your child is already an adult.

5.

The Best Parenting Philosophy Is Wise Application of Wise Principles and Practices

No extreme parenting approach—authoritarian or hands-off—should be regarded as a wise method of parenting. Alas, a happy medium style of parenting between these extremes, while sounding good in theory, does not provide specific guidance to a parent on how best to raise a child. The parenting philosophy presented in *Wise Parent* advocates knowledge of all the wise principles and practices laid out in its pages as well as their regular application in ways most suitable for your particular child at his or her particular stage of development.

Such an integral approach calls on you to develop a well-informed and long-term perspective on raising children as you seek to apply your wisdom in day-to-day life. Try to bring more awareness and insight into your parenting experience and resist the tendency to run on autopilot. Ask yourself periodically whether your parenting is balanced, or whether you need to place greater or lesser emphasis in any given area.

Keep in mind that your task is not to craft a masterpiece out of your child, but to give your child the best foundation you can, and hope and trust that your child will find their path through life as they mature. Have faith in the wisdom of these teachings, as well as confidence in yourself and in your child.

6.

Know the Goals of Wise Parenting and Turn Them into Your Daily To-Do List

Your primary task as a good and wise parent is to know what your child truly needs and to provide for those needs. Ultimately, what your child needs most is that which will enable them to reach adulthood with good physical health, psychological well-being, moral insight, social abilities, positive values, good habits, and useful life skills.

Realize that even if you are guided by these goals and have a strong sense of duty about achieving them as a parent, you are still not guaranteed an ideal outcome! Such an outcome, however, is far more likely, and that alone justifies the effort involved in following the path of wise parenting. If your child grows up to become a capable adult and a thoroughly decent person, he or she will be a source of immense joy and blessings to you—and be of benefit to society as well. And isn't that, after all, what you would like the children of other parents to grow up to be? So remember the goals of wise parenting, and use this book to help turn those goals into your daily to-do list.

7.

Your Own Upbringing Should Not Be Your Main Reference Point in Parenting

In raising your child, do not be guided primarily by what you remember liking or disliking about your own childhood. If you grew up in relative poverty and your central motivation now is to give your child the opposite of what you had, you may end up overly pampering and spoiling your child. If you always wanted to pursue some dream but never did, pushing your child to pursue the same dream may well go against their nature. If your parents were very strict with you, being very permissive with your child will surely cause its own problems.

The world today is different from what it was then, your child is different from who you were then, and you as a parent are different from your own parents. The only constants then and now are the wise principles and practices, which serve as better guides to good parenting than your own childhood memories, wishes, and impressions.

8.

Other People's Opinions about Your Parenting Skills Don't Matter Much (but Take Note Anyway)

So long as you are following the wisdom teachings contained in this book and are reevaluating from time to time how you apply them, you should not be overly concerned with what relatives, friends, or strangers think or say about how you are raising your child. Some people may sincerely believe they know better than you what's good for your child, even if they're basing it only on their own experience as parents and not on a careful assessment of your child. In any case, do not resent their attempts to make their contribution, learn what you can from them, and simply take it on faith that they are all well meaning. Certainly don't view it as an affront to your ego or an undermining of your parental authority, and don't confront them defensively or offensively unless truly necessary.

Though you know best the specific challenges faced by your child, and in your hands lies the primary responsibility for raising your child, do take into consideration suggestions by others to make sure your current parenting path is not way off course.

9.

Parenting Requires Making Personal Sacrifices—Know Which Ones You Need to Make

Although being a devoted parent does not mean neglecting other essential aspects of your life, it does mean making the necessary sacrifices to allow you to do a good job of raising your child. Sacrifices that you may regard as substantial—like setting aside large sums of money so your child can attend a prestigious college—might not be the ones that are most important to make. Sacrifices may, instead, come in unexpected forms, such as giving up some of your own character weaknesses, including perhaps your tendency to indulge in negative moods, to always look for immediate solutions to possible problems, or to seek excessive control over people and events. Even learning to live in peace with the fact that as a parent you may never receive the credit, thanks, and appreciation you think you deserve is a sacrifice of sorts.

Other sacrifices are more obvious, such as the need to cut down on time-wasting personal activities that you may have grown attached to: watching too much television, talking at length on the phone, or surfing the Internet for hours on end.

In short, make the necessary and sufficient sacrifices in your social, professional, and personal life in order to apply these one hundred principles and practices effectively—all in the spirit of selfless love and dutiful maturity.

10.

Your Own Difficulties Do Not Justify Straying from the Path of Wise Parenting

If you are going through tough times, whether it be work problems, marital problems, health problems, financial hardships, or any other difficulties, realize that you cannot simply set aside the principles and practices of wise parenting. You should apply as many of them as possible as often as possible, even under difficult circumstances, and make adjustments and arrangements as needed while you address your hardships. Never just tell yourself it is inevitable that your child will suffer until things sort themselves out in your life. Rather, make it a point to keep your child's well-being in mind throughout the difficult period.

If you continue to show your child love and affection, spend as much time with them as you can, and shield them from the more extreme manifestations of life's tribulations, you can trust that they will be quite all right.

11.

Never Despair over Your Child or Be Too Hard on Yourself

Parenting is challenging enough even without the added frustration and despair you feel when things don't go as smoothly as you'd like. Don't conclude that you are failing as a parent just because your child is difficult or leaves much to be desired in your eyes. Remember that your child is their own person with their own complex mind that cannot be made to work according to your will. Take heart from the fact that there is more than a narrow developmental window during which you can have an influence on your child. *Throughout* the time your child is under your care, your persistence in following the lessons of wise parenting will sow the proper seeds, even if your child seems unreceptive to your positive influence. Sooner or later, your child is likely to understand that your efforts were noble and your advice sage.

When your child is going through difficult times and there is nothing else you can do but love, pray, and be present, recognize that your child must walk down their own path and that no human life is without periods of pain and adversity.

12.

Don't Remain Mired in Guilt

Parental guilt can take on a life of its own if it is not dealt with prudently and promptly. Any real or perceived wrongdoing on your part can trouble your conscience and hold your attention captive. For mistakes that are more than just minor, you should indeed feel remorse and seek to set things right, just as you should always learn from your mistakes and try not to repeat them. But to let guilt turn into an emotional habit robs you of the self-compassion you deserve as a conscientious parent. To allow guilt to develop into a lingering wound also interferes with the work of wise parenting. If you do not confront your parental guilt constructively and with full awareness, you may end up permitting your child to do things they should not be doing, all in order to assuage your feelings of guilt.

Keep in mind that guilt over matters that can no longer be remedied in the present or over vague matters—such as believing that you may not be living up to someone else's expectations—is more destructive than helpful. And many common sources of guilt are entirely unjustified, such as feeling a sense of guilt for having to work outside the home, or for saying "no" to your child when you are right to say it. Similarly, if you are unable to attend many of your child's athletic events or other such activities, do not feel guilty and think you are somehow depriving them of a parent who is fully there for them.

Let guilt find a temporary home in your conscience only if it should, but then release it into the past as you resolve to be more constructive and move on to meet new challenges in life.

13.

Know When You or Your Child Needs Extra Help and Seek It Out

There will be times when you will need to get competent advice or help—medical, financial, psychological, and the like. Whatever help you or your child requires, seek it without delay and without shame or embarrassment.

If your child has special needs, address them patiently. If you are too emotional about the situation, your good judgment may suffer and adversely affect how you evaluate which course of action to take or which expert advice to follow. Take some time to reflect quietly on the matter without undue pressure or alarm. Connect with other parents who may share your particular challenges in order to aid you in assessing various options to meet those challenges.

It will help put things in perspective if you also remind yourself that with or without special challenges, your child's complete development requires the application of all the wise principles and practices. So don't focus narrowly on any area of difficulty without keeping in mind the bigger picture of your child's integral development.

Understand that some problems need to be addressed as they arise, and some need to be lived with and studied for a period of time before any action should be taken. Some problems go away on their own and some are understood later as having been mislabeled as problems in the first place. Your experience and wisdom as a parent will grow over time, and your ability to recognize what is before you will increase as well.

14.

Don't Equate Parenting with Friendship

If you ask yourself what the duties of a good parent include—to provide, protect, nurture, discipline, love, mentor, and the like—you will find that there is only a *partial* overlap between good parenting and good friendship. Parenting requires much more of you than a friendship does! Parenting is a relationship not between peers or equals, but between a responsible giver and one who depends on—and is in great need of—what is being given.

Seeking to be your child's close friend may be a good impulse, but not to the detriment of more important considerations. Let your child have friends their own age, and stick to your parental duties.

15.

Don't Strive to Ensure Your Child's Constant Happiness

Your primary job as a parent is to seek and provide what is good for your child. If, instead, your focus is on whatever will make them happy at any given moment, you will not be fulfilling your primary parental task. Realize that many things that are good for your child, including telling them "no" and setting boundaries, won't make them happy at that moment. Such unhappiness will surely pass away quickly. However, if your child is used to getting from you what they want when they want it, as adults they will find it very difficult to remain happy dealing with a world that is much less amenable to their personal whims and fancies.

If you strive to ensure your child's constant happiness, you will also impede their development of effective mental and emotional coping skills, as you'll be denying them the opportunity to practice on their own the abilities called for in handling everyday sources of frustration. This doesn't mean you should avoid comforting your child and reassuring them that "this too shall pass" when they come to you sad or crying. But if you also help your child learn how to live in peace with things they cannot change, you will be doing the most to help ensure their happiness later in life.

16.

Don't Strive to Secure Your Child's Constant Love and Approval

Do not be driven by a desire to be loved by your child or to gain their approval. If you fear that your child will express a dislike for you—even a temporary dislike—you will never put proper restrictions on their conduct or chastise them when necessary. If you let them develop bad habits or allow them to take part in unwholesome activities because you fear that if you stand in the way, their love for you may diminish, by the time they grow up, they might actually come to resent you! They will realize that their entrenched bad habits could have been prevented if only you had done your parenting job with more important considerations in mind than merely attempting to secure a child's love and approval.

17.

Better Person, Better Parent

Use parenting as an opportunity to grow as a person, knowing that this will make you a better parent and your child a better child. Parenting will surely teach you that you are not perfect and will clearly highlight for you some areas where you could improve yourself. But don't agonize over the fact that you cannot always live up to your highest ideals or always act wisely. Parenting is an art that calls for your own growth in wisdom, virtue, and skill, which you can begin to work on this moment and continue day by day. In fact, such growth is the best guarantee you have of doing a good job as a parent! So work on your own development as a person, and seek to enhance your strengths and reduce your weaknesses.

Know your own psychological shortcomings, and try not to have them play a negative role in your functioning as a parent. Discover areas where your remaining patterns of immaturity should give way to more responsible patterns of behavior, and embrace such development. If you notice yourself turning more bitter, cynical, or jaded as a parent, work instead on being more positive, hopeful, and renewed in spirit.

To avoid feeling overwhelmed by the needs and pressures of modern life, become more organized, improve your time management, keep a to-do list, rank your priorities, and adopt better daily habits and routines. Lead a wholesome, balanced, and healthy lifestyle characterized by the ideal of simple living and high thinking, which will give you more energy for parenting and less stress at the end of each day.

Always keep in mind that taking care of only your child and not yourself—including your growth as a person and the well-being of your body, mind, and soul—is not good for you or your child.

18.

The Better the Marriage, the Better off the Child

A stable and loving relationship between the parents is highly conducive to the optimal development of the child. If it is clear to a child that their mother and father get along with one another and jointly look after his or her well-being, the child is spared many psychological problems that could hinder their healthy development. A child also gets a valuable opportunity to observe up-close how an adult man and an adult woman relate to one another in a committed relationship.

Always invest in your marriage and in your spouse and take the time necessary to deepen and enjoy your mutual relationship. Make it clear to your spouse that you support them and value their various contributions, and don't be quick to complain about any perceived lapses. Try your very best to consistently show them respect, courtesy, and affection, and also be sure to point out your spouse's good qualities in your child's presence. Try to avoid ever undermining your spouse's authority in the eyes of your child and always wish for a good relationship between them. Most importantly, resolve all marital disputes in ways that do not jar your child's sensibilities.

Discuss candidly, but fairly, all issues with your spouse, including those relating to the raising of your child, and work closely together toward achieving common parenting and relationship goals.

19.

Maintain a Positive Home Environment

Try to make your home the sanctuary of every family member, with a prevailing atmosphere of love, joy, trust, cooperation, and harmony. Minimize bringing into the home the concerns, stresses, and energies of the outside world, especially those related to work. Realize that your state of mind in your child's presence directly affects their own state of mind and that it influences the quality of your mutual interactions. If you can institute a daily period for quiet activities and one day a week as a day of rest, all family members will have the opportunity to slow down their normal pace, calm their minds, and uplift their spirits.

Try also to resolve family disputes well before bedtime, and don't let them build up and fester over days and weeks. But it's equally important to learn to live in peace with honest disagreements! Preach and practice the ways of respectful discussion and civil debate, avoiding unneeded escalation and heated arguments. Don't let a day go by without there being some expressions of humor, fun, and playfulness in the home, which can work wonders for diffusing tension.

While even the home décor can play a role in creating the right ambience, it is principally the attitudes and actions of all those in the home that create the proper atmosphere.

20.

Spend Plenty of Time Together

Spend a great deal of time with your child, from the day they are born till the day they leave the nest. Otherwise, it is not possible to adequately apply many of the principles and practices of wise parenting. For a child's optimal development, it is best to have the mother (traditionally) be at home with them much of the day during their early years. Work it out as well so that you, your spouse, or ideally both of you eat daily at least one meal together with your child, even into their late teens.

When you are at home with your child, be available as much as possible and allow them to interrupt your leisure or work activities if it seems important to them. It is this availability on your part, coupled with your willingness to spend a considerable amount of time together, that conveys to your child most fundamentally how much you value them.

Don't presume that only educational or fun activities constitute worthwhile time spent with a child. In fact, *any* time a child spends with parents who follow the path of wise parenting is quality time. So when you go out shopping or on errands, take your child with you if possible, even if it's inconvenient. If you are assembling a store-bought item of furniture or doing some special work around the house or yard, see if your child is willing to join you. Though you or your child might not actually *feel* that every moment spent together is precious and irreplaceable, remember that it is indeed so.

21.

Be Observant and Attentive

Even when your child is young, do not assume that you can have only partial presence of mind when you interact with them. While many of their concerns may seem petty compared to adult concerns, realize that for a child, learning to cope with life is still a developing skill that requires parental monitoring and nurturing. You need to play a vital role in this process by being present, alert, and responsive to your child. You need to be attentive and attuned. Seek to know what is going on in their mental and emotional interior as well as in their outward behavior and environment. Examine what is in plain view and probe deeper by asking questions. Note your child's current state of mind, discern the needs of the moment, and adjust your approach accordingly. Observe your child closely so you can better help them cultivate their strengths and address their weaknesses.

Remember that your child's perceptions are very different from your own. Therefore, try your best to see through your child's eyes—how he or she sees the world—so you can understand them better and relate to them more effectively and appropriately.

22.

Always Consider Age Appropriateness

Firmly keep in mind the concept of age appropriateness, which means never failing to take into account your child's present level of development. This applies not only to whatever you expose your child to, but also to what you expect of them. Always say, do, expose, and expect according to your child's age, capacity, and current ability to assimilate knowledge and meet standards of behavior. Never forget that different standards apply to children and adults. Your child may not know any better at this point in time, nor could they reasonably be expected to know any better. Therefore, make only those demands you're fairly certain your child can meet at their current level of development.

23.

Learn about the Developmental Stages of Childhood and Adolescence

On your way to becoming an adult, you went through all the developmental phases of childhood and adolescence. However, as you were not yet in possession of sufficient self-reflective abilities or a broader frame of reference, you did not gain substantial insight into the process of child development. Naturally, the best way to learn about this process up close is to raise children. But reading a few good parenting books and obtaining good advice from wise and experienced mothers and fathers (including, of course, your own) will make you that much more knowledgeable and prepared.

Keep in mind that all children start at square one, and helping them navigate step-by-step into adulthood can be done with greater ease if you have a good sense of what to expect along the way. If, for example, you tell a young child not to be sloppy, but they are at a level of development where the necessary motor skills, awareness of danger, and concentration are not sufficiently developed to avoid being sloppy, your words will have very limited effect and may even cause further frustration for you and your child.

So, take the time to learn about the physical and psychological development of children and the various stages children go through from infancy to their late teens. Identify the stage at which your child is currently, and recognize what is typical behavior for that stage and what requires closer attention. Be mindful also of what is conducive to your child's healthy development at that stage and what isn't. Just remember that children, like adults, do not develop without periodically taking one or two steps back.

24.

Each Child Is Unique

Think of your child first and foremost as a distinct individual—not as an extension of yourself. Don't habitually compare them to their siblings, other children, or to adults including you or your spouse. No two children will ever be exactly alike, just as no two adults are alike. Each child has his or her unique psychological makeup with inborn inclinations that continue to manifest over time. Each child grows in the various lines of development (cognitive, emotional, interpersonal, etc.) at a different pace.

Your child's disposition may or may not be similar to your own: introverted or extroverted, mellow or energetic, dreamy or practical, and the like. You will need to adapt in some ways to suit your child's temperament—for example, in the manner in which you communicate or in the kinds of games and other leisure activities you do together.

In following any parenting advice, always consider how best to apply it to your individual child at their particular stage of development. As you come to know your child's nature, tailor your style of parenting to work well with it. This will help ensure that your child is being more receptive and that you are being more effective.

25.

Boys and Girls Are Different

Where applicable, recognize the differences between raising boys and raising girls, from the toys and kind of play they more naturally gravitate toward, to their emerging psychological and biological differences. For example, most boys will be more physically aggressive, so their aggression will need to be kept in check, though do allow some permissible outlet in such things as rough-and-tumble play. Boys also tend to be more competitive and more driven to prove their competence to others. Most girls will be more emotional and more prone to being overwhelmed by their emotions. They are more likely as well to overwhelm others by their emotions, which you should also address. Girls also tend to have their mood and self-esteem be influenced to a greater extent by their subjective sense of their physical appearance and by the strength of their interpersonal relationships.

As a parent, you should take into consideration such differences to help you relate to your child better and to help your child accentuate the positive aspects of their nature and learn to minimize the negative aspects. Keep in mind, however, that within both sexes there is a wide range of individual expression. Some boys and girls will grow up to be tough, military-type persons and some will be very sensitive poet types.

26.

Each Parent Can Emphasize Different Aspects of Parenting and Allow for Distinct Gender Roles

Both parents need to show consistency and agreement between themselves in the key areas of childrearing, especially in enforcing ground rules of proper behavior. Both parents should also avoid any sense of parental competition in their relationship with their child or allow the child to play one parent against the other. It is, however, desirable for the mother and father to each emphasize different parenting roles and make their own unique contributions. For example, a child commonly benefits from a more nurturing and accepting mother and a more challenging and autonomy-encouraging father. By mere exposure to the distinctive feminine and masculine aspects represented by each respective parent, a child also gets to absorb important behavioral cues and valuable insights into human nature.

If you are a single parent, while you do need to fulfill both gender roles as best you can, try to have one or more trusted close friends or relatives of the opposite sex help with that task.

27.

The Family Is One Unit

Make it clear through words and actions that the family is one cohesive team whose members are honest with one another, affectionate toward one another, and share what they have with one another. Every member of the family should feel a strong sense of belonging to the family. Every member should be taught to show concern for the health and happiness of every other member of the family and have a sense of obligation to provide emotional support and practical assistance when needed.

Develop family traditions, customs, and rituals, and make them part of everyday life. Have all family members rejoice in celebrating together holidays, birthdays, rites of passage, and other milestones, as well as commemorate events tinged with sadness. Try to convey the importance of simply appreciating and cherishing the time spent together as a family.

28.

Avoid Favoritism, Minimize Jealousy, and Mediate Sibling Conflicts

Though there are numerous benefits to raising multiple children and growing up with siblings, having more children in the home also means having more conflicts to manage. Realize that if you avoid playing favorites in the way you treat your children, there will be much less sibling rivalry and jealousy.

While you do not need to feel the exact same loving way toward each of your children, you should never convey to a child your greater or lesser love for them compared to their siblings. You can cater to each child's specific needs without seeking to follow a rigid equality in treatment, but also don't let any child develop an ongoing sense that they are the ones who usually get the short end of the stick. Give each of your children due attention and dedicated time alone with you, even those who don't seem to need it as much.

When conflicts that demand your involvement arise between siblings, properly mediate them in a way that makes clear the underlying principles guiding your mediation, and apply your principles consistently and fairly. Be sure, however, to also encourage your children to negotiate among themselves and to settle their differences on their own.

Have private conversations with each child to address particular gripes they may have against their siblings or against you. Convey to older children that you expect them to act more maturely than their younger siblings. Specifically, they should try harder to avoid unnecessary conflicts with their younger siblings, yet, if they see their siblings doing something dangerous, they should stop them and inform you about it immediately. Make sure, though, that the older child is not bossing around their younger siblings, as this could lead to long-lasting resentments.

Reduce unnecessary sibling tensions and divisions, and when harmony is lost, work wisely to restore it.

29.

Understand and Utilize the Power of Impressions and Associations

Because children are considerably more impressionable than adults, it is essential that they be exposed to things that will leave good impressions on them and shielded from things that will leave bad impressions. Impressions are formed when the child perceives something in their environment that leaves an emotional imprint on them. Just what kind of impression they form is based on the nature of what they observe and their interpretation of it.

Impressions work like seeds that sprout character tendencies, which, in turn, give rise to behaviors. For example, if your child sees how much your volunteer work makes you happy, they will form an impression that helping others is a source of personal satisfaction and will be more likely to help others as well. If they see you frequently resorting to alcohol in order to wind down, they will form an impression that such substances are important for relaxation.

The younger the child, the deeper the impressions sink into their mind, and thus the more opportunity you have to create long-lasting positive impressions. Just before your child goes to sleep—when they are very receptive—create good impressions by reading stories or by offering insights that are helpful for their proper development.

Also make frequent use of the power of associations—the power of creating links between two ideas—to convey to your child how one virtue promotes another. For example, link for your child the concept of moral behavior as being a good source for feeling self-worth, of inner strength being a basis for resisting unhealthy indulgences and negative peer pressure, and of perseverance being a foundation for accomplishment. Such mental and emotional links will also replace less beneficial associations they may get from their environment.

30.

You Are Always Teaching by Example— Realize It!

Whenever possible, teach by good personal example. Why? Because your child will learn by the example you set, whether you are intending for them to or not and whether you are setting a good example or a bad one!

Teaching by personal example is your most potent parenting tool. It is what you embody and demonstrate that your child observes and imitates. Recognize that over time, your child actually absorbs many of your virtues and vices of character by merely being with you and seeing how you act and react. Your day-to-day conduct in your child's presence greatly influences their psychological and moral development as well as their present and future well-being. If, for example, they see you treating your own parents or even strangers with respect, patience, and affection, they are more likely to develop these virtues and end up treating you and others the same way. If they see you lying to others, they are more likely to lie to others in turn and probably to you as well. It is best if your child sees you doing what you want them to emulate, including the simple things such as reading, exercising, and eating properly. With children, even more so than with adults, actions speak louder than words.

This doesn't mean you should be a paragon of perfection. In fact, if your child sees you learning from your own mistakes as you cope with challenges and frustrations, this will provide them with valuable lessons. But if your attitude is, "Do as I say, not as I do," it will only be a matter of time before your child neither listens to you nor does what you want them to do. So be a good role model and set a personal example of the values, traits, and behaviors you preach.

31.

Patience, Patience, and More Patience

One indispensable quality a parent should develop in themselves is patience—lots and lots of it, and then some. Remind yourself often how vital this virtue is, both when your patience is being tested and at all other times! It helps to remember that you were once a child, a young adolescent, and an older but not yet fully mature teen. Realize how rapidly children grow and change, and how a more mature stage of development is just around the corner for them.

Have compassion for your child and cultivate a spirit of forgiveness and understanding. Appreciate how they, too, have to cope with fears, desires, frustrations, disappointments, uncertainties, and an abiding sense of dependence. Have faith that your wise application of wise principles and practices, done steadily and patiently, will have your child emerging whole from the many stages of growth they will undergo. Thanks to patience, you too will emerge intact and better off in all respects.

32.

Keep Your Anger in Check

Do your utmost to control your temper and not let it boil over or even reach the boiling point. Be slow to anger and quick to cool down if you do get angry. Don't use swear words with your child, don't rant and rave, and always watch your tone of voice. When you do raise your voice, don't yell or scream, and certainly never cause your child any physical pain. It is your job to de-escalate and diffuse difficult situations—not to make them worse! You can often diffuse a difficult situation by offering your child a diplomatic out from the corner they backed themselves into. Also, don't hesitate to be the one who takes the first step in easing tense moments and mending strained relations.

Sometimes it is better not to react at all or to underreact—to give your child a knowing look or a look of disappointment, or to express in few words how their conduct is affecting others. If you overreact too often, the entire dynamic of the relationship between you and your child will change, and your child will begin to hide more and more things from you.

Even if you are able to control such overt manifestations of anger, don't let anger simmer to the point where much of what you tell your child is conveyed with antagonism, as if you are holding a grudge against them. Realize that deeply hurtful words ("Why can't you be like your brother?"), broad generalizations ("Everything is your fault," "you always," "you never"), and aggressive vibes can have a worse effect than yelling or even spanking, so take a time-out yourself if necessary. Reflect on the true source of your anger and don't misdirect your anger at your child. Use anger for show to get a point across that doesn't otherwise get across, but don't let anger take control of you.

33.

Keep Your Worries and Fears in Check

Parental anxiety is part and parcel of being a parent, but it's still worth minimizing because it makes no positive contribution to your well-being or to that of your child. Endless worrying drains you of physical, mental, and emotional energy and diverts your attention away from the present, where it is needed most.

Worrying excessively about your child's lack of ability in any particular area while they are still in the process of growth and development turns you into a hostage of your own expectations. Having your awareness be narrowly focused on any one overriding fear (for example, that your child will not do particularly well in school) prevents you from keeping a proper perspective on meeting your various obligations as a parent. Undue fear over any aspect of your child's life could even push you into taking unreasonable or rash actions.

If your growing fear is actually well-founded, then you should pay more attention to that area of concern. But also keep in mind that showing your child that you are greatly alarmed or panicked by anything in your life or their life (for instance, in connection with a doctor's visit) is highly unsettling to them.

Let go of as many worries and fears as possible about things you have little or no control over—or things that are really not that important—and show more faith, courage, and equanimity in your attitude and behavior.

34.

Help Your Child Cope with Their Fears

Children, especially young children, need to feel safe and secure in their environment. If your child expresses their fear of the dark, monsters, or bad dreams, tell them that unreal dangers are made to appear real and large by one's imagination. Show them reassuring affection and certitude that they are perfectly safe. Conveying such certitude is particularly important regarding their fear of abandonment and separation from you.

Increasingly affirm to your child your belief in their inner strength and capacity to handle fears with courage and reliance on their many inherent abilities. If your reassurances are not sufficient, give your child time to grow in courage. Do not, for example, force a child of any age to remain alone in the house if they are very afraid to be left alone. Also, realize that as a child matures, some of their fears may go away, while other fears will begin to take center stage, especially those arising from the need to fit in socially with peers.

Do not compound your child's fears by telling them that the world is a scary place with dangers lurking around every corner. Neither should you instill fear in your child over various minor dangers or the panic du jour circulating in the news, or expose them prematurely to overly unsettling or frightening media stories and images. Nor should you let your child suspect that something scary which may affect them is shaping up behind the scenes. And certainly don't use fear as a primary technique to get them to do what you want!

Help your child cope with their existing fears and don't create unnecessary new ones. A child who grows up with few unnecessary fears and with the courage to face their fears not only enjoys greater psychological well-being, but also forges ahead more confidently to meet life's challenges.

35.

Be Positive and Happy—or at Least Act It—as Much as Possible

Parents who are generally happy and show it are more likely to have a child who grows up happy, as children take many of their emotional cues from their parents. Children also find it easier to listen to the advice and requests of a parent who is usually cheerful and pleasant. In fact, nearly everyone (not just children) feels uplifted in the company of someone who is upbeat and joyful. So, work on having a positive disposition and on finding and radiating more of your joy—being bubbly or jubilant is not what's required of you.

Enjoy your role as a parent and take pleasure in interacting with your child. Show some lightheartedness and good cheer not only when you are in a great mood, but at many other times as well. Laugh at their jokes and make plenty of jokes yourself. When you see your child at the end of their school day, always show them that you are very happy to see them.

Children are known for their joy of life. Imagine the dampening effect a frequently sullen and sour parent has on a child and you'll need no convincing of the need to try and act happy, even when there is much that could be weighing you down.

36.

Show Your Child Warmth, Affection, and Love Daily

Always make your child feel wanted and welcomed. Express your warmth and love plainly and abundantly—the more the better. Show them physical affection every day—hold them, embrace them, kiss them—and tell them you love them.

Even when circumstances seem to prevent you from expressing your love outwardly (for example, when your child is testing your patience), try to feel your love inwardly. It should be very clear to your child by your words and actions that your love is not dependent on them meeting any particular expectation or fulfilling any particular duty. Love for children needs to be unconditional.

Love also means wanting what is truly good for the one you love, and what is truly good for a child is a parent who does not shy away from any parental responsibilities. So love unconditionally but wisely, and you will see your child flourish. Accept the fact that the amount of love and joy you *get* from your child will vary from time to time and from child to child.

37.

Don't Spoil or Overindulge Your Child

If your child usually gets most of the special treats they want, then either your child happens to have very reasonable wants—or you are overindulging them! Whether you are spoiling your child in order to increase their happiness, to get them to be more cooperative, to secure their love, or perhaps to relieve your own parental guilt, remember that good intentions do not necessarily translate into good outcomes unless one's actions are guided by wisdom.

Whether your child is asking for candy, games and toys, or fun experiences, don't overindulge them too often. If you overindulge, they will under-appreciate. Even if the toys are educational and activities bonding, maintain a sense of moderation in providing out-of-the-ordinary experiences.

If your child wants the same things that their friends have and you do not want to buy those things or can't afford them, explain that it is best for every child to be happy with the many good things they already possess rather than be envious of what their friends have. Also tell them that most children in the world have only a small portion of what *they* have, and no one can have everything their heart desires. Encourage your child to appreciate and make the most of what they have, and teach them to find interest and joy even in relatively mundane things such as reading, interacting with a pet, or honing a skill. Keep in mind that to never overindulge your child is not good either, because there's a right time for that too. And giving your child anything they *actually* need (in whatever measure they need it) should not be considered as spoiling at all.

Also, remember that allowing overdependence on material comforts is a form of spoiling, so make sure your son or daughter is not so used to luxurious convenience that they lose their stamina to tough it out, for example in camping or hiking. Creature comforts are nice to have, but a temporary separation from them should not translate into restlessness or unhappiness.

38.

Be the Primary Decision Maker

Throughout the parenting years, you will need to make countless decisions for your child. Although you should gradually be giving your child increasing freedom to make many of their own decisions, it is your responsibility to make all the important decisions for them. Regularly offer your child the opportunity to choose from a few options acceptable to you, but never burden your child with making any particularly consequential decision—even if they are eager to make it. A child can neither be expected to decide as wisely as would their adult parent, nor is it reasonable to have them bear the consequences of decisions they should not have made in the first place.

The principle of ultimate parental responsibility also holds true when relying on the opinion of experts, who should never be thought of as having the final say on matters relating to the raising of your child. Listen to the experts' advice, consider it carefully, but make your own decisions, relying on sound knowledge, reason, experience, and parental intuition.

When your child has left the nest, they can make all their own determinations. Until then, don't delegate your role as the primary decision maker to anyone.

39.

Provide for Your Child's Physical Needs

Fulfill your role as a provider by offering your child a safe home environment, adequate and nutritious food, comfortable clothing and bedding, and everything else that will make them feel that their basic physical needs are being met. As it happens, a well-fed and well-rested child develops fewer behavioral problems and is an easier child to raise!

The duty to provide will naturally involve spending more and more money on your child, so earn enough to meet all their basic needs, cut down on frivolous expenses, and save enough to safeguard your family's well-being in case of an emergency. Take steps to make certain that if something happens to you or your spouse, your child will continue to be well cared for. This may include preparing a will and getting a life insurance policy to adequately provide for your child's needs in such eventualities.

Always remember, however, that being a good provider should never come at the expense of being an ethical role model. No fancy toys, extravagant celebrations, or expensive vacations can ever make up for the sense of shame a child will feel if their parent conducts his or her life or business affairs without morals.

40.

Nurture and Monitor Your Child's Health

Have your child be under the care of a trusted pediatrician and make sure they get regular checkups, necessary vaccinations, and prompt medical attention and medication as needed. When your child is sick, spend more time with them. Treat them tenderly and calmly, reassure them and cheer them up, and accommodate their need to be distracted from their discomfort.

Become well informed on matters of child health and general health. Ensure that your child's daily diet is drawn from all five basic food groups—from various nutritional sources within each group—based generally on a food pyramid guide. Greatly limit junk food and sugary beverages, explaining to your child that the primary purpose of food is to build and maintain a strong and healthy body. But don't forget flavor and variety! Broaden your child's palette gradually by learning to cook dishes from several foreign cuisines, and get your child excited to try new food items. Be especially creative with vegetable preparations and persist in offering them—baked in a pot pie or as toppings for pizza; plain or pureed in soups; cooked with various spices and sauces; cut fresh in interesting shapes with different dips and dressings. Also make sure your child eats a variety of fruits in a variety of colors daily.

Instill in your child a love of physical activity. Exercise will allow them to spend some of their abundant energy and will help them stay in a healthy weight range. Teach your child that fitness consists of aerobic capacity, muscle strength, flexibility, and balance, and have them participate in sports and other physical activities to develop all four aspects.

Also, teach your child the various habits of cleanliness and hygiene, but don't be too fussy about such matters, particularly in their first few years. Early exposure to less-than-perfect cleanliness actually builds strong immunity!

41.

Protect Your Child from Physical Harm

One of your primary duties as a parent is to protect your child. The younger the child, the less developed is their perception of danger, and therefore the more alert and vigilant you should be to ensure their physical safety and freedom from injury. Notice in advance those situations when even a moment's distraction on your part is too long (for example, when giving your baby or toddler a bath), and maintain heightened awareness and complete presence of mind during such times. It takes a young child only a few seconds to put in their mouth a food item or other small object that can pose an immediate choking hazard.

Childproof your house room by room and cabinet by cabinet to prevent access to kitchen knives, weapons, plastic bags, matches, medications, detergents, and the like, by moving them higher up or locking them away. Teach your child safe handling habits of sharp, hot, and fragile items, as well as proper handling of pets. Instruct your child on road safety, and remind them periodically to always follow the rules of the road. Make sure your child uses protective gear during sporting activities.

Pay the greatest attention to protecting your child from more immediate and serious harm, but also be mindful of long-term dangers, such as the harm caused by excessive exposure to the sun, to unhealthy air quality inside the home, to lead and mercury, and to dubious chemicals in various food items and household cleaning products.

42.

Safeguard Your Child's Innocence

Protect your child's innocence from adult subject matters and indulgences. Mind your language around your child and avoid speaking to other adults on topics not suitable for children if your child is present. Realize that a child becomes increasingly less innocent through exposure to, followed by fascination with ideas, images, and actions that are more base and crude. The fact that such things exist in the world doesn't mean your child needs to know about them sooner rather than later! Showing an eight-year-old boy an R-rated violent movie, for example, is irresponsible. Allowing a pre-teen or young teenage girl to wear sexually suggestive clothing is also irresponsible.

Childhood is fleeting as it is. By rushing it, you deprive the child of a sufficient opportunity to build a strong foundation of self-awareness, self-control, and discernment between right and wrong. So shield your child to a large extent from adult issues and problems until you think your child is ready to confront them.

43.

Shield Your Child from Popular Media and Overconsumerism

Because children are so impressionable and because media stories and marketing messages can create such strong impressions, it is vital that you monitor what your child is being exposed to and that you shield them accordingly. If popular culture and the prevailing social norms were actually conducive to raising good children, your job as a parent would be much easier. So long as they are not, you have to serve as the gatekeeper. This includes monitoring your child's television watching, Internet surfing, music listening, and video game playing.

Prohibit video games with antisocial themes and music laced with profanity. Restrict your child's access to unwholesome content and adult contact on the Internet by setting up proper software filters. Also, don't allow your child to have a TV in their room until their mid-teens (if ever), and greatly limit their exposure to TV advertisements by minimizing their exposure to commercial TV programming. Having your child grow up thinking they really need all those advertised toys and snacks will undoubtedly make them more restless and less happy!

As your child matures, give them more access to media content, but also provide them with the proper context to judge what is good and helpful and what is to be avoided because it is harmful. Specifically, remind them that what is being shown on television is neither a complete and accurate portrayal of real life nor a depiction of what is necessarily desirable. Tell them as well that advertisements seek in various ways to whet our appetites and increase our wants without limit. It is only when your child internalizes those lessons that their exposure to this medium becomes a safer proposition.

44.

Get to Know Your Child's Friends—but Interfere Only When Necessary

Always know where your child is, who they are with, and—to the extent necessary and possible—what they are doing. Emphasize the value of connecting with others in good friendships, encourage your child to seek friends who serve as good influences, and help steer them to good company. Recognize, however, that you will never have a full say in the matter, so try at least to get to know their friends.

If one of their friends has some obvious negative traits or habits, give your child the freedom to associate with that friend, but point out exactly what they should not be learning from that friend and why. Such conversations can also be used as an opportunity to remind your child that any of their friends may at some point pressure them to do something wrong, and that during such times, courage is necessary to resist these pressures and avoid doing things they will later regret. Acknowledge that peer pressure and the desire for peer approval are often powerful forces, but ultimately every person decides whether or not to be swayed by such forces.

If, however, one of your child's friends is overwhelmingly a bad influence, then greatly minimize or forbid contact—even if your child gets very upset at you for it. Only you as the parent know the likely long-term negative consequences such associations can have for your child, so stand your ground.

45.

Let Your Child Play Every Day—and Join Them in the Fun from Time to Time

A happy childhood involves a good amount of fun and games, so let your child play every day and enjoy toys, games, sports, and plenty of unstructured playtime outdoors. Because children often take their play seriously, when you join in from time to time, follow along in earnest, but try to use the opportunity to work with them on such skills as strategizing, taking turns, and adhering to the rules.

Strengthen the bond with your child by engaging in many different activities together that are fun for them: playing make-believe, doing crafts, going on outings and picnics, visiting amusement parks, star-gazing and cloud-watching, cooking, singing, and anything else that would bring joy to their life and add many wonderful memories. Family vacations in particular tend to leave a child with lifelong memories, especially if they involve travel to places that are quite different from what the child is used to at home.

As your child matures, also be sure to introduce them to great movies and great music of many different genres, including the classics.

46.

Have Reasonable Expectations

The younger your child, the fewer expectations you should have of them. Whatever expectations you do have, always make sure they are reasonable. To expect a young child to sit still at the dinner table for a long meal is unreasonable. To think that a child can stop being shy by simply asking them to is also unreasonable. It is especially unreasonable to have specific expectations about relatively unimportant things, for example that your child will participate in a particular sport, play a specific musical instrument, attend one college over another, or end up working in a particular profession. Your child may not be good at some things you would like them to be good at, but may be very good at other things—the specifics should ordinarily not be of concern to you. In fact, a child who is made to feel that they can never live up to even just one parental expectation, is made—unfairly—to carry a heavy burden.

The only long-term expectation and thus the only future image you should have of your child is that of a mature and psychologically healthy adult with the values, character, and judgment that enable a satisfying and meaningful life.

47.

Good Communication Is Vital

Be a good communicator with your child. Be straightforward and plainspoken. Make sure you have your child's attention before you attempt to get an important point across. At times, appeal more to your child's mind, and at other times appeal more to their heart. When appropriate, explain your reasons and express your feelings.

Teach your child that communication consists of conveying clearly, listening well without interrupting, and responding properly. Conversing often with your child is the single best way to develop their communication skills and to maintain good and open lines of communication. Keep in mind that if you want your child to open up to you about any particular subject, you may first have to open up to them about the same subject with personal stories of your own.

When your child is talking to you, try to look at them to make it obvious that you are fully present and attentive. Listen with empathy and an open mind, and strive to ascertain (if unclear) what it is they are really trying to say.

Encourage your child to ask for clarification if they don't understand something and not to be timid in seeking knowledge and understanding. Encourage them as well to tell you if they are ever being bullied or otherwise mistreated by anyone.

In relating to your child, remember that they are always drawing cues from your verbal and nonverbal communication, so pay close attention to your own reactions to their words and actions.

48.

Answer Your Child's Questions Thoughtfully

Your child will ask you many questions, some of which will be difficult to answer. Make sure you do not give curt answers or discourage your child from asking in the first place. Never say to them, "How could you be thinking such things?" but rather address their concerns with an attitude of openness and understanding. Realize that if your child doesn't get answers from you, they will likely get them from someone or someplace else—or from their own fertile imagination!

Unless you are in the middle of something pressing, be patient enough to give your child well-thought-out answers, at least to their more important questions. You can also revisit your answers with amendments and additions if some additional useful point comes to mind. Sometimes, though, it is better to merely steer your child to the answers so that they can feel they have arrived at the answers on their own.

Your child will not forever think of you as all-knowing, but your relationship will benefit greatly if your child always sees you as a valuable source of knowledge and wisdom and knows you gladly share it.

49.

Correct Yourself When You Make a Mistake

Every now and then you will make a mistake in how you treat your child. It could be in what you said or how you said it, in what you didn't say but should have said, in what you did, or in what you didn't do but should have done. Whenever this happens, you need to tell your child simply, "I'm sorry," and proceed to set things right. Doing so is more important than you may think: Your child will learn that honesty, humility, and making proper amends are essential virtues, and that because you practice what you preach, you are even more trustworthy. In addition, for occasions when you opt not to apologize, your child is more likely to believe that you were right in what you said or did!

If you speak or act in a way that serves as a bad example for your child, besides apologizing you also need to tell them, "Please don't think based on what you've heard me say or seen me do that ...," and then mention the negative life lesson they should not be learning from your bad example. For instance, say, "Don't think that mommy and daddy don't really love one another," "that using profanity is appropriate," or, "that aggressive outbursts are OK."

Learning to restore confidence and harmony by apologizing and clearing the air will also ensure that good feelings prevail and relations between family members stay strong.

50.

Build Mutual Trust

Build trust with your child and nurture a close bond. Let your track record clearly show that you are honest, trustworthy, and reliable. Try to avoid giving your child reason to believe you are hiding important things from them or else they may begin to question your honesty. When you make promises to your child, try your very best to keep those promises. If you are also able to show your child that you can accurately predict likely consequences of actions and events you bring up in discussions with them, your child's trust in you will grow.

From time to time, demonstrate to your child that their word is good enough for you to fulfill your end of a bargain first, before they have to fulfill theirs. Convey often that you believe in them and that they have your full backing and support for all their positive endeavors. Ingrain in your child the understanding that they can always confide in you and turn to you for advice and solace because you love them, respect them, and only want what is good for them.

51.

Be a Mentor

Realize that, for all intents and purposes, you are also your child's guru! One of the primary roles of every parent is to convey to their child valuable wisdom about life—the knowledge necessary for living life well. A wise mentor is not someone who simply allows their child to learn the most important lessons on their own, often by having popular culture supply the answers. Instead, a mentor gives the one under their care ample guidance and instruction drawn from the mentor's own life experience and heritage—and from the wise principles and practices presented in this book. A parent-as-mentor helps their child form the basic mental structures of understanding about the world around them and their place in it in a way that fosters a healthy, growth-oriented view on life.

When a child is still young, teaching wisdom means emphasizing simple concepts of virtue as expressed in real-life situations. When a child is more mature, you can discuss various aspects of life in a broader, or more abstract, context. Doing so will help your child develop a deeper and more philosophical outlook on life and will allow them to reflect on their own values. For example, "Don't hit your brother," can, in later years, turn into discussions about violence being justified only in self-defense or defense of other innocents against substantial harm. "Share your toys and play fair with your friends," is broadened in the course of time to dialogs about one's sense of fairness and generosity. "Don't worry too much about being popular in school," can later be part of conversations on the folly of pursuing fame at the expense of one's values, and on the fundamental difference between mere fame and actually having important accomplishments to one's credit.

Teach your child appropriately at every stage of their development, even as they naturally learn on their own, and help them integrate both sources of knowledge.

52.

Pass on Worthy Traditions

Pass on to your child traditions that are beneficial to their character development and to the forming of their personal and communal identities. Whether such traditions are cultural or religious, ethnic or familial, local or national, keep in mind that continuity of tradition should only be maintained for those traditions that are still in line with wisdom and virtue and not merely for the sake of continuity. Your foremost goal is not to make your child a proper member of a specific group, but a human being of good character, good values, and good conduct. Group traditions can help put that goal in context, accelerate its achievement, and otherwise enrich your child immensely, yet what is most essential should always take precedence over what is secondary in importance.

53.

Expose Your Child to Heroes and Other Positive Role Models

Children need to be inspired, and their idealism needs to be nurtured. A child's potential is unleashed more readily and fully when they become aware of other people who have already unleashed their own potential. Therefore, expose your child to heroes and other good role models—in stories, in movies, or in person—and explain to your child why such figures are inspirational. Teach your child that heroes are admirable men and women who have pursued noble goals and ideals and were able to achieve them through courageous effort, often after making substantial personal sacrifices and resisting various pressures.

Pay greater attention to role models who have exhibited one or more essential virtues and have lived their lives well, rather than to those who are known for some specific practical achievement. Your child may not discover or invent anything of note, but their achievement and contribution will be great if they grow up to become a thoroughly decent person—someone with good values who utilizes for good ends whatever talents, abilities, and resources they happen to have.

54.

Expose Your Child to Religion and Spirituality

If you are a person of faith, you sense that the highest purpose and meaning in life is to be found in religious or spiritual ideals. You recognize that all aspects of living, including childrearing, should be informed by an all-encompassing worldview. By exposing your child to religion and spirituality, you awaken their heart and mind to deeper insights and set them on a course toward greater fulfillment in life. When you emphasize the cultivation of virtues in their upbringing, you not only ennoble their character, but you also promote their lifelong spiritual growth.

Tell your child they have a soul that needs to be nourished, just like the physical body needs nourishment. Give your child a sense of the sacredness of life, of the divine essence in every human being, and of the holiness of God. Allow your child to experience the wondrous and the magical, the mythical and the mysterious. Teach them to pray and ask them to have faith in a loving God who is always with them, though God is non-material, like love itself.

Pray for your child daily, which will also infuse you with love, patience, and an understanding of what is most important. Worship together in the home and go together to a house of worship, where a sense of community can be nurtured. Celebrate religious holidays and highlight some fun elements that appeal to children, such as gift-giving and gift-receiving, special foods, ceremonies, songs, and get-togethers. Share the great edifying stories of your religious tradition with its many virtuous role models. Tell your child about the wisdom in scriptures and about the clarifying and uplifting words of the wise.

Give your child the advantage of a religious foundation and a broad-minded spiritual outlook, and as they grow to appreciate the tangible and intangible benefits it provides, they will not abandon it.

55.

Teach—but Don't Indoctrinate

Pass on to your child knowledge and wisdom, virtues and values, traditions and customs, but don't indoctrinate them in any area, including religion and politics. Indoctrination means forcing an airtight belief system on your child. Not indoctrinating means giving your child room to believe that even though you regard what you convey to them to be proper and true, if they don't accept it fully or even if they argue with you about it, you do not think less of them or necessarily condemn their own views. Such a measure of tolerance and broad-mindedness on your part will lead your child to respect you and your views more genuinely, and will foster in them a deeper spirit of inquiry.

56.

Allow Your Child Broad Self-Expression

Give your child considerable freedom to express themselves in non-harmful ways. If they wish to personalize the décor of their room, accommodate them within reason, even though their tastes and interests are likely very different from your own. As they get older, allow them to choose what clothes they wish to wear, except when their choice suggests bad judgment rather than merely bad taste.

When your child's behavior is a bit hyper, annoying, silly, or otherwise less than ideal, don't always attempt to restrain their behavior or stifle their energetic and spontaneous spirit. Raising children is not about trying to raise saints! In fact, if you don't allow any expression of even some crude elements of their nature, those elements will merely settle in their subconscious and may resurface later in life in harmful and shadowy ways.

Emphasize to your child your expectation that they control their behavior in matters of greater importance and during more formal settings, help them find positive outlets to channel their drives and tendencies, but otherwise be quite permissive. Give your child enough space to figure out who they are as they go through the various stages of development and to express their personality and range of feelings in nondestructive ways. Providing them this space will also minimize their inclination to be rebellious as adolescents.

57.

Give Your Child the Liberty to Make Some Mistakes and to Cope with Setbacks

To be watchful, protective, and involved in your child's life is a commendable duty, but to be overprotective and to want to shield them entirely is counterproductive. If you are constantly troubled by the prospect that your child will experience any obstacle, disappointment, or other difficulty (or, for that matter, get any scratch or bruise), you are being overprotective. It is not beneficial for a child to be shielded from every mistake, loss, or failure they might experience. A child should realize that such occurrences are all part of a normal life, and that one needs to develop the necessary coping skills to handle such challenges and to always pick oneself up and continue on with life.

Teach your child that mistakes and setbacks provide excellent opportunities for learning and growth and are often stepping-stones to success. Your child will also learn firsthand that experiencing the consequences of one's poor choices can increase one's motivation to act more sensibly in the future. Such insights will help your child build resilience, determination, and confidence, and will allow them to enjoy greater emotional and mental well-being throughout their life.

58.

Don't Be a Taskmaster

In whichever way you expect your child to help out around the house, instead of merely presenting it as their duty, try to make it a positive experience and show them you value their contribution. It is best, in fact, not to demand your child do more than a few basic household chores. After all, household chores are primarily your job as a parent. Too much friction—for a relatively small benefit—can be created in the home if a parent insists that their child do many cleaning and organizing chores, and the child is resistant. Such friction can breed resentment, and the child fails to absorb the life lesson the work was supposed to instill in the first place! Overemphasizing your child's responsibility for doing their share of household work can also detract from your focus on their more important obligations—in the realms of moral and social development and in their schooling.

Accentuate the positive aspects of everything you would like your child to do and make tasks, chores, and duties that might seem not so pleasant sound more appealing. Make clear the many advantages of doing one's duties and thereby increase your child's motivation to do them. From brushing one's teeth to completing a school project, try to highlight the benefits, the fun, the challenge—including by making a game of things when your child is young—even if you ultimately have to insist they do what is required of them.

59.

Distinguish Between Requirements and Preferences

Convey to your child that good character, good conduct, and fulfillment of one's basic duties are what you value most. Your child will be able to tell what is most important to you by simply noticing what you give primary attention to in the course of daily life and what issues you bring up most often in conversation.

Recognize the difference between essential requirements and your personal preferences, the former being high on the list of what is ultimately important and the latter being much lower. Learn not to push your preferences too much! You may prefer a different hairstyle for your child, but how crucial is it really? Whether their room is especially tidy is also not particularly important compared to so many other things. Realize as well that there is little need for nagging—either the matter is not very significant and you should avoid making repeated requests, or the matter is significant and you should be much more decisive, insistent, and firm in your words and actions.

Be very selective in what you wish to be more demanding about, and pick your battles wisely. If you don't make too many demands of your child, it is also easier and more justified to insist on the more important ones.

60.

Set a Few Simple Rules and Clear Limits

Don't lay out needlessly restrictive, complicated, or unnecessary rules for your child to follow. Whatever rules you have, make them clear and simple. Make the consequences for breaking the rules also clear, and apply the consequences accordingly and consistently.

Have your child mind their language, demonstrate their good manners, and avoid disrupting other people's enjoyment in public. Depending on your child's age, place limits on the type of leisure activities they engage in and the time spent on them. If your child protests, get them to understand that one cannot simply disregard one's obligations in life in the name of pursuing any activity, however enjoyable or worthwhile the activity might be.

Strictly forbid physical aggression such as hitting, biting, and pulling hair, but don't label as violence every physical contact on their part, especially in the case of boys. Also, you shouldn't just tell your child not to do something you find unacceptable. Instead, say, "Don't do this, but here is what you can do that I don't mind," and proceed to point out an acceptable alternative. When seeking to prevent your child from engaging in certain behaviors you find particularly objectionable, don't do so by issuing such dramatic, fanciful, and repetitive warnings that you end up causing your child to develop a fascination with trying out those particular behaviors.

Keep in mind that just because you may not have always abided by your parents' rules when you were a child, that this somehow absolves you from insisting your own child always do so. Your authority to set rules and enforce limits is a function of your role and responsibility as a parent, not of your personal history.

61.

Provide Correction and Discipline

When your child does not meet the basic standards of respectful behavior, self-control, and conformance with the ground rules and limits you've set, correct them, scold them, and even punish them if necessary. However, always do so with a sense of appropriateness and proportionality. Whatever correction or discipline you impose has to be measured and thoughtful rather than instinctual, the obvious purpose being not to hurt your child but to help them learn and grow. Never chastise just to reassert your parental authority. Instead, do so only following a clear and intentional violation of your reasonable expectations that are also well known to your child. Be sure your child understands exactly why they are being chastised, and whenever possible, chastise them only in private to avoid embarrassing them unnecessarily.

Making severe threats and yelling at your child in response to a behavioral problem may create a worse, long-term problem instead. Your goal should be that your child will learn to behave well not only when they are under your direct supervision, but also when you are not around them. So don't be harsh when they fail to meet your expectations—after all, you do not want them ever to give up hope of improving their conduct. Neither should you be critical without also being constructive, nor should you be frequently critical about relatively trivial matters. And certainly don't adopt extreme punitive measures while hiding behind some general notion of tough love. Do insist, however, on standards of proper behavior, because an unruly child who grows up to become a highly undisciplined young adult is a menace to themselves, to those around them, and often to society at large.

62.

Have a Large Repertoire for Handling Misbehavior

When your child misbehaves, realize that there are many tools available to you to get them to correct their misbehavior. If one approach doesn't seem to work any longer (or never did), experiment with variations or try entirely different approaches. Opt for a mild and gentle approach at first, and if that doesn't work then become stricter. However, go back to the gentle approach if it has been awhile since your child last misbehaved.

Don't use only the standard retorts, "Just do it," and, "Because I said so." Say something like, "Do it for me like I do things for you," "I know you can think of at least one good reason yourself," "You know me well enough that you should trust me," and so on.

Try reasoning with your child and explaining to them with added clarity. Try asking in different ways and with greater urgency. Use a more determined tone of voice to signal that you mean business.

Even when you do need to take action, consider a variety of approaches, such as temporarily denying privileges, temporarily showing reciprocity in behavior or attitude, using time-out and sending the child to their room for a brief period, or telling the child what they need to correct as you hold them and look them in the eyes. Spanking should not even be considered unless the misbehavior is very dangerous or harmful and all other methods of discipline fail repeatedly. And even then, do so with the utmost self-control, without force, and largely symbolically.

Try as well to involve your child in finding solutions and in formulating suitable agreements to solve their own behavioral problems. And always keep in mind that whenever possible, it is better to show your child appreciation, give them encouragement, and offer incentives and rewards for good behavior, than to later have to resort to admonishments and punishments in order to address their bad behavior.

63.

Be Consistent

Even though you ought to have many methods for changing your child's misbehavior, you should demonstrate a high degree of consistency in formulating expectations, setting boundaries, and applying rules. Your child will get confused if you frequently change the rules or their application, or the consequences for their violation. If you are not consistent in such matters, the necessary and valuable lessons you need to impart to your child will simply not register in their mind or will register with conflicting messages.

Children need a sense of order and rhythm in their lives with some fixed rules and regular routines to enable them to make better sense of their environment and reduce their feelings of anxiety and restlessness. A high level of stability, regularity, and consistency on your part will allow your child to feel more secure in your care, knowing they have predictable standards to conform to.

Realize, however, that because your child does not yet know what is truly in their best interest or what is necessitated by the constraints of reality, they will go to great lengths and try their hardest to get you to change your mind, be inconsistent, and allow them to have their way. While you should give your child the freedom to attempt to manipulate you into being inconsistent—often by utilizing their knowledge of your own soft spots and weaknesses against you—give in only if doing so would not likely lead to bad outcomes.

64.

Deal with Your Child's Anger Appropriately

Set limits to your child's expressions of anger, but also allow them to express it, including by raising their voice every now and then. What you should rarely do, however, is yield to their tantrums! Recognize that during such times it is especially important to keep your cool and to be lovingly firm. Tell your child that Mom and Dad don't behave this way and that you expect them not to behave this way either. Tell them that wants, as opposed to needs, have no limit and nobody gets everything they want all the time. If you give in to their tantrums, they will have more of them and will pull them like a lever to get you to relent every time. As you contain each tantrum patiently and intelligently, keep in mind that it is preferable in the long run if you teach your child how to cope with their frustrations in a more constructive and mature way.

Whenever your child gets angry, gauge the situation with full awareness to determine how best to respond in this particular instance—compromise or insistence, humor or seriousness, more discussion or less discussion. Certainly don't take personally every hurtful statement your child makes or every episode of acting out. But do try to acknowledge rather than ignore or condemn your child's feelings, to indicate to them you understand their frustrations, struggles, and desires, even as you then explain the limitations of reality. For example, say, "I know you really want me to buy this gift for you now, but the best I can do is to try to buy it for your birthday," or, "I understand how frustrated and angry you are that I'm not letting you play some more with your friends today, but you've hardly studied for your exam tomorrow."

A toddler or young child's tantrums can often be cut short (or even prevented entirely) with a clever parental distraction of the child's attention. But as your child matures, you should discuss with them how anger can easily cloud one's good judgment and how it can often lead to hurtful words and actions. A person cannot give anger free reign but must restrain it, help it subside, and then reflect on it constructively.

65.

Express Disapproval for Specific Conduct—but Don't Withdraw Your Love

Do not use giving of love and withholding of love (whether through words or actions) as a means of controlling your child's behavior. Children should never feel rejected by a parent, and a parent who withdraws his or her love—even if temporarily—signals a rejection to the child. But you can and sometimes should express your disapproval and displeasure until your child corrects specific actions or words that don't conform to the ground rules you've set. And most of the time, it is not even necessary to hold back your approval until your child shows full compliance—it is often enough if your child demonstrates an earnest effort to improve.

66.

Don't Blame or Burden Your Child Needlessly

Don't blame your child or allow them to believe blame lies with them for things that are not their fault. If you make them feel blameworthy for things they did not cause, they will begin to think of you as arbitrary and unfair and may start to disregard the rules and expectations you've set. Also don't burden your child by taking your personal frustrations out on them or by weighing them down with issues and concerns that are not theirs to tackle. And certainly don't make your child feel—directly or indirectly—that it is their responsibility to make you happy and fulfilled. Specifically, you should not act as if the child's successes and failures are also your own. Always remember that you have your specific duties and burdens and your child has theirs.

67.

Never Ridicule or Humiliate Your Child

Just as you expect your child not to make fun of other people in a mean-spirited way and would prefer they always show sensitivity to other people's feelings, don't act in a callous manner toward your child. Never humiliate, ridicule, or taunt your child in an offensive way, especially not in front of others or on matters they are very self-conscious about, such as their physical appearance or their basic competence. Children are much more sensitive than adults and are liable to be deeply hurt by such callous treatment.

If you enforce discipline or make legitimate demands, your child may be temporarily upset with you. But if you speak or act in a cruel or humiliating way, your child will harbor long-lasting bitterness toward you and will develop inner wounds that may not heal for a long time.

68.

Reinforce All that Is Good in Your Child

Every aspect of your child's character and behavior that you reinforce is likely to take stronger root, especially when the reinforcement comes soon after the behavior. Use this simple psychological principle of reinforcement to help your child persist in any good behavior they exhibit. Give frequent validation, positive feedback, and ample encouragement. Note their sustained efforts, good conduct, good judgment, and worthy accomplishments. A child who learns through experience that their good behavior elicits more attention from their parents than their bad behavior is more likely to behave well in the future.

Keep in mind that giving positive feedback and encouragement is actually more effective in the long run than giving high praise, because it is more reflective of what your child can realistically expect to encounter later in life. Reserve giving high praise for a younger child, and as your child gets older, do so more for their substantial accomplishments. Do not, however, consider good grades and practical achievements as being more praiseworthy than good character and good conduct! As you know from interacting with your own peers, being a good person and a good friend is more praiseworthy and often more difficult than developing any practical skill or attaining any particular achievement. So tell your child you are proud of them—for all the right reasons.

69.

Nurture Your Child's Curiosity and Help Them to Explore Their Talents and Interests

Develop your child's natural curiosity about the world and nourish their desire to learn and grow in knowledge. Get them to be more fascinated by how things work and encourage them to pursue their curiosity. Share in their delight of discovering something new and show excitement in their presence at learning fascinating things yourself. Be enthusiastic when you teach your child new skills, tasks, and games.

Convey the importance you place on acquiring valuable knowledge and tell them that doing so is a lifelong pursuit. Take your child to various museums and exhibitions, buy them science kits, and give them informative books on a variety of subjects to see what areas captivate their interest. You will find that as adolescents grow to recognize their own aptitudes, they are typically drawn more to scientific and mechanical subjects or to the humanities, arts, and aesthetics.

Expose your child to a variety of hobbies, see which ones they like, and support these the most. Realize, however, that it is perfectly normal for a child to change their various likes and dislikes periodically and to abandon most of their hobbies sooner or later.

Such broad and sustained exposure will allow your child's interests and talents to emerge over time. Their self-understanding will also increase, and their habit of pursuing knowledge and putting it to good use will deepen.

70.

Read to Your Child and Get Them to Read Early on

Children learn more from stories than from abstract ideas, so read to your child regularly and tell them stories of family lore or other tales that will inspire them, entertain them, educate them, pique their curiosity, or otherwise leave a good impression on them.

As soon as your child is able to read, encourage them to do so as often as possible, even if for only ten minutes at a time. To make reading more inviting, start them with books that are beautifully illustrated, and have them read while you are also reading your own books or magazines nearby.

In their pre-teen and teen years, make sure your child is exposed to some of the great children's books of all time. If they do not respond well to any of them, attempt to find a genre or author that they do like, keeping in mind that boys and girls may enjoy entirely different subject matters.

Your child will undoubtedly benefit greatly if the reading they do is not just for homework, but also for their own pleasure and personal enrichment.

71.

Be Involved in Your Child's Education

Always play an active role in your child's education. Convey some of your own knowledge of history, geography, civics, culture, and any other useful subject with which you have familiarity. Present them with simple computation questions and increase their vocabulary daily. Consider introducing them to a foreign language when they are young—the best time for learning a second language.

If you have a say in what school your child attends or what teachers they study under, pick the best ones, of course, but also consider whether those choices are a good match for your child's specific needs.

Instill a love and joy for learning. Remind your child periodically that any of the major fields of study can be interesting if approached with curiosity, attention, and enthusiasm. Teach your child effective learning skills and habits—including not having distractions while studying—to enable them to learn any subject well. Help them avoid undue stress before exams by getting them to understand that study and preparation serve as the best antidote, and that repeatedly reviewing lessons and drilling skills are key to learning and memorization. Ask them what topics they are studying in class and get them to summarize for you something interesting they learned recently.

Insist that your child do their homework, but if they need extra help, make sure they get it. Obtain a good understanding from your child's teachers about particular academic or behavioral concerns they may have with your child, but don't be distressed if your child seems to falter. Deal patiently, lovingly, and wisely with all such challenges.

72.

Emphasize Good Effort Usually, Excellence Sometimes, Perfection Rarely

Instill in your child the idea that they need to exert sustained effort in their mastering of skills, in their character development, and in their schooling, but don't frequently insist on excellence or perfection. Show them again and again how repeated practice in any given area leads to improvement, and how goals that are set can be met if one puts in a good effort to attain them. You should encourage your child to strive for excellence—meaning a high degree of competence—in a few key areas, but don't overemphasize such a high standard unless your child seems inclined to it.

Perfection is rarely a desirable expectation of a child except when it is clearly defined and the child can attain it in any given area without experiencing excessive levels of stress. It is fine to tell a young child that coloring completely inside the lines of a coloring book amounts to perfection, but increasingly complex tasks become less amenable to perfect performance.

If your child demonstrates a remarkable talent, then do nurture it to the highest levels. However, to expect your child to maximize their potential or to worry a great deal about your child being at some competitive disadvantage while they are still adolescents is not very sensible.

Your child should develop faith in their ability to exert sustained effort and to see good results follow, but they should not be driven by outside pressures to meet very high standards without an accompanying inner drive for such high achievement.

73.

Increase Your Child's Attention Span and Have Them Work on Long-Term Projects

Good concentration is one of the most important human abilities. It is necessary for proper comprehension, retention, and application of knowledge and skill in all areas of life. Increase your child's attention span by having them engage regularly in activities that require prolonged active concentration. Whether it is by completing a jigsaw puzzle, organizing a dollhouse, or sitting down for thirty minutes to read a book, build up your child's ability to remain focused for increased periods of time without requiring ever-changing external stimulation. When your child is absorbed in such activities, try not to interrupt their concentration.

Also, have your child work on projects that take hours, then days, then weeks, then months to complete. This will teach them that patience and perseverance are necessary for accomplishing one's goals. Get your child to grow a plant from seed until it bears fruit, build a model by following instructions until it is fully assembled, or any other undertaking where the final result comes only after diligent and protracted effort.

74.

Help Your Child Deal with Their Boredom Constructively

Though you may find it convenient at times to keep your child busy by having them watch television or play video games, these forms of entertainment are often superficial solutions to alleviate boredom. Extensive exposure to such sources of sensory stimulation will cause your child to become more restless, and soon enough most other activities will seem boring by comparison!

Encourage your child to immerse themselves in activities that include an inner dimension of ideas, imagination, and creativity, such as reading, doing crafts, practicing a useful skill, or working on a hobby. Give your child games and toys that can be augmented by the player's own imagination, and be sure to have them make the most of their toys before rushing to buy them new ones. Also, encourage your child to participate in after-school programs, but don't let overscheduled structured activities serve as the only solution to boredom.

Express to your child the idea that if they learn to be more interesting themselves—that is, more curious about the world and more sociable with others—they will find more things to be interested in and will never have to worry about being bored.

75.

Teach Your Child about Human Nature

Your child will benefit greatly from having an ever-expanding knowledge of human nature. The better they understand themselves and others, the more they can live in harmony with others and with themselves. Over time, introduce such concepts as thought and emotion; awareness and attention; memory and impression; desire and need; instinct and intention; tendency and habit; motivation and willpower; mood and temperament; the conscious and the subconscious; the waking, dreaming, and deep-sleep states of consciousness; imagination and creativity; inspiration and intuition; attitude and perspective. Tell your child that these and other elements of human nature are universal, and that even many of the specific instincts, desires, habits, and the like are actually common to all people.

Also explain to your child that all human beings have both virtues and vices of character, which represent respectively better and worse ways of relating to others and to oneself. Virtues increase goodness and happiness and vices increase selfishness and sorrow.

Convey to your child that beyond any accomplishment they achieve in the world, they will grow most as human beings if they work on developing a strong and wise mind and an open and loving heart.

76.

Instill in Your Child Good Morals and Develop Their Conscience

Cultivate in your child a clear-cut understanding of right and wrong. A child will not develop a solid moral foundation if the moral principles conveyed to them are finely nuanced, non-definitive, or otherwise unclear. Start with this simple version of The Golden Rule: Do not do to others what you do not want done to you, which means one has to refrain from words and actions that harm others. Make abundantly clear to your child that their moral obligations include not taking what belongs to others and not being dishonest. As a positive obligation, ask your child to be kind and helpful to others in word and deed.

Tell your child stories and show them movies that reinforce morality and good conduct. Follow up by asking them questions to ensure they have absorbed the key moral lessons. Also, teach your child aphorisms on virtue and ethics even if they don't yet understand the aphorisms' full significance. Tell your child that in every area of life a person should be ethical. If your child is able to make the connection between doing the right thing and feeling good about it, they will more readily apply their growing moral understanding. But make clear that they need to do what is right regardless of whether they feel like it or not, because morality is based on standards, principles, and obligations—not on personal feelings. The same is true for asking your child to consider their motives when they speak or act but emphasizing to them that good behavior counts more than merely having good intentions.

Check your child's moral compass by discussing matters that have ethical implications—stressing less the big moral issues and more the questions of day-to-day ethical conduct. Help your child develop their conscience to recognize when they have said or done something wrong, to feel remorseful, to apologize, and to make amends.

77.

Teach Your Child about Good and Evil in the World

Well before your child reaches their teenage years, teach them about good and evil in the world. Explain *good* as conduct that helps others and increases others' happiness. Explain *evil* as conduct that causes great suffering and unjustly ignores the rights and freedoms of others. Point out that tyrants, oppressors, terrorists, and some criminals do evil acts, and suggest that the reason they do so is because—in wanting to get their way at all costs—they either don't listen to their conscience, or they follow a bad belief system that justifies their bad behavior, or both.

Reassure your child that good people far outnumber people who wish to do such harm, and that good overcomes evil. However, in order for good to triumph, good people must not be complacent, but must stand up in defense of themselves and in defense of other innocents.

Expose your child to books and movies that illustrate the nature and danger of evil ideas and actions—both works of fiction and of historical fact.

78.

Monitor and Minimize Your Child's Character Flaws

Even if you think of your child as your "little angel," keep in mind that all human beings come with various weaknesses, character flaws, and bad habits—and can easily develop more of them! To prevent these patterns from becoming increasingly entrenched in your child's personality, you will need to monitor and correct your child when they exhibit such behaviors. Make the more significant vices of character a priority: Tell them to be less self-centered (the natural state of almost all young children), not to be mean or vengeful (typical when they feel angry or jealous), and not to lie or cheat (common when they wish to protect themselves or get their way). But don't label your child based on any of their flaws, or else they may become attached to the label and embrace it as part of their self-identity. And instead of strictly condemning the negative aspects of your child's character and building up in them a large shadow of shame and fear, teach them to become more aware of their own impulses and behaviors and to recognize for themselves what their good and bad tendencies are.

When your child makes a poor character choice, tell them to learn from their mistake but not to wallow in feelings of regret or guilt. You can help your child make better character choices by giving them rational reasons why vices are detrimental. For example, tell them a person who lies gets in ever deeper trouble and loses a great deal of credibility, which is difficult to restore. But teach your child as well that any weakness of character is more easily overcome by developing the opposite strength of character (courage in the face of fear, humility in place of arrogance, generosity instead of greed) rather than by wrestling with the weakness directly. By developing virtues and through repeated good conduct, one's negative tendencies diminish on their own.

79.

Teach Your Child Impulse Control, Delayed Gratification, and Self-Discipline

Emphasize to your child the vital importance of controlling one's impulses, resisting instant gratification, and exercising self-discipline. These abilities are key to your child's character development, future happiness, and success in life!

Help your child associate self-control with strength. For example, practice together not indulging in some treat for a period of time to see who is strong in resisting temptations. Also, offer your child a larger reward if they agree to forego a smaller one that is due sooner. Explain that exercising self-discipline builds willpower, and with greater willpower they can realize more of their dreams.

Before your child reaches adolescence, educate them about the nature of addiction. Describe it as indulging an urge without demonstrating control, moderation, or insight into what is good for one's well-being. Tell them that cigarettes, alcohol, and drugs are bad for their body and mind and are therefore strictly prohibited. Let them know that many adults who use such substances develop a destructive addiction and end up regretting ever starting down that path. This is all the more true in the case of an alcohol or drug addiction, which can destroy one's relationships and one's life.

Teach your child to always prefer a life of moderation and balance, avoiding harmful influences along the way and resisting the impulse to be reckless or extreme in anything they do.

80.

Teach Your Child about Sex

Convey to your child timely, suitable, and easy-to-comprehend information about sex—either when you think they need to know certain facts or in response to their specific questions. Ensure that a healthy and comfortable atmosphere about such matters exists in the home, but also ensure that all family members speak and behave in a manner that is desexualized when relating to one another (with the exception, of course, of the parents relating to each other).

Teach your young child about improper sexual touching, and ask them to tell you if anyone ever does so to them. Give your child useful information about their own biological and psychological changes at appropriate times, especially before and during puberty. Tell them it is perfectly natural to have sexual urges and to feel attraction and curiosity to be close and intimate with the opposite sex. Inform your daughter that most boys have a considerably stronger sexual urge than girls do and are more easily aroused visually, and therefore it is important not to tease or provoke boys in this way. Tell your son to treat girls with respect and to never do anything against a girl's will.

Let both sons and daughters know about the great harm that comes from sexual promiscuity, including the many sexually transmitted diseases, unwanted pregnancies, and lasting emotional scars.

Encourage them to be abstinent or to have sexual intimacy only in the context of a meaningful, long-term relationship.

81.

Help Your Child to Sharpen Their Awareness of the Outside World and to Deepen Their Self-Awareness

Encourage your child to expand their awareness of the outside world and to gain insight into their internal motives and moods. To develop their power of external observation, ask your child to notice a particular detail or aspect of a person, animal, or object you think they may be unaware of, such as a butterfly that is resting on a leaf or a picture that is hanging crooked on a wall.

Encourage your child to introspect and be mindful of their inner motives. Ask them periodically, "Why do you think you did that?" which will go a long way toward increasing their self-awareness. If your child plays overly-stimulating video games, ask them to notice how such play affects their state of mind—whether, for example, it is making them more impatient or aggressive.

Also teach your child about moods and how they affect one's view of people and events. Tell them that even though bad moods tend to go away on their own, one can and should make these moods pass more quickly to ensure they don't develop into a negative attitude toward others. Teach your child that not only moods change, but one's perspective changes as one grows and matures.

82.

Prepare Your Child to Be Increasingly Independent

Children start off life being entirely dependent on their parents. Over time, they naturally and very gradually grow to become more independent. So long as you realize that one of your primary aspirations as a parent should be that your child will reach adulthood as a mature person capable of meeting his or her own needs, and so long as you deliberately help this maturation process along, your child will develop a substantial measure of independence and self-reliance.

If you already give your young child plenty of attention yet they still crave more, tell them occasionally to entertain themselves for a while. Let your child also deal independently with some challenges and problems if doing so doesn't cause them too much stress. If they say to you, for example, that another child is not being nice to them, don't necessarily offer detailed advice on what they should do. Instead, consider first saying you believe they can handle the situation on their own, and then follow up by asking how they actually dealt with it.

Gradually give your child more space by becoming less involved in the minutiae of their day-to-day life. When friendships with peers become increasingly important to them, understand that their greater independence requires they spend less time with you. But convey early on that personal independence also means being responsible enough to resist the negative effects of peer pressure and herd mentality. Point out that not everything their peers do or popular culture promotes is consistent with good judgment and good values, and that they should exercise their independence to be free of any negative influence—whatever its source may be.

83.

Teach Your Child about Duties and Responsibilities

Emphasize the importance of fulfilling one's duties and responsibilities. Make your child in charge of various things small and large, depending on their age and capacity. Help them to understand that fulfilling duties is truly in a person's best interest, because a person who regularly does so grows in skill, confidence, and virtue, and gains the trust of others. Whether it is the duty to respect their parents, to do their homework, to clean up after themselves when asked, or to act with fairness toward others, when your child fulfills these and other duties, express your appreciation and tell them how happy and proud you are that they are acting maturely.

Instill the idea that one should focus on one's obligations, especially one's duties toward others, and not develop an overriding sense of entitlement centered on one's perceived rights. Explain that whining, feeling self-pity, thinking of oneself as a victim, being a sore loser, and being easily offended are common feelings, but are immature and unhelpful feelings nonetheless, which should be gotten over quickly before they develop into resentment, jealousy, anger, hatred, and vindictiveness.

Tell your child that being a mature adult largely means handling duties and responsibilities well in all spheres of life, instead of making various excuses for not doing so. Ingrain in your child the understanding that they need to take responsibility for their actions and reactions, because one always has a choice in how one behaves.

84.

Help Your Child Develop Self-Confidence and a Healthy Self-Image

Strengthen your child's sense of self-worth by pointing out their many inherent abilities—to think for themselves, be creative, make progress in the areas they pursue, be of service to others, and the like. Suggest that by applying these inherent abilities, their self-confidence will naturally grow.

Give your child the opportunity to develop their confidence and sense of pride through personal achievement that is unaided by you or others. Bolster their self-confidence by reminding them that their capacity to learn is limitless, and that even if they don't know something or do a poor job at some task the first time around, they can always learn and improve. A child who independently accomplishes any task they previously believed was beyond their capacity gets a substantial boost to their self-confidence. Recognize that healthy self-esteem can never be based on receiving empty assurances from others that one is perfect just as one is. Instead, it should be based on developing faith in one's inherent potential, on remembering one's past accomplishments, and on cultivating a desire to continue to grow and achieve.

Help your child form a healthy self-image with regard to their body as well, which is especially important in the case of girls. Tell them they are beautiful! Tell them to think well of their body and to ignore comments by children who ridicule the appearance of others just so they can feel superior about themselves. But also convey to your child that lifelong beauty is seen primarily in their attitude, character, and behavior. Taking better care of the body and wearing clothes that are more flattering is important and can certainly add to one's beauty, but most adults value inner beauty more than external looks. Teach your child that external beauty is largely in the eye of the beholder.

85.

Instill in Your Child Positive Thinking and a Positive Attitude

Infuse your child with optimism, positive thinking, and a can-do attitude. Explain that optimism does not mean believing that things will necessarily turn out the way one would like them to. Rather, it means believing that good outcomes are likely to result from good effort and good attitude, and that some good can be made to come out of any situation.

Tell your child that life is characterized by frequent change, and therefore a person should be able to adapt to change and continue to move forward. Let your child know that every person goes through tough times, although it is best to minimize their occurrence by acting more wisely in the first place. Whenever sad events happen or pain and suffering are experienced, one needs to face them with awareness and learn whatever lessons they can offer. When your child feels sad because of loss or disappointment, encourage them with the words that life goes on and that they should try to feel hopeful about the future and not dwell in the past.

Teach your child that life presents everyone with various problems and difficulties, but that it's best to view them instead as opportunities and challenges and address them with a sense of adventure and confidence in one's abilities. Tell your child that while self-doubt is normal, a person should rise above it, be constructive, and use positive thinking to work on challenges with the faith and hope that they can be overcome.

Instill in your child the idea that they can attain success in their endeavors by being diligent and persistent—and by maintaining a positive and enthusiastic attitude. These qualities will enable them as well to influence others to be more positive, enthusiastic, and successful.

86.

Teach Your Child to Relate Well to Others and to Be a Good Team Player

Help your child develop the ability to get along well with other children. Teach them to play nice, to communicate their thoughts and feelings respectfully and tactfully, and to show regard for the wishes of others. Nurture a disposition to see some good in all people, rather than to always look for faults in others or to speak ill of them. Tell your child to act friendly toward all their schoolmates, not just their friends, and certainly to never bully or otherwise mistreat another child. Emphasize the value of maintaining harmonious relations with others, which often calls for sharing and compromising, and of restoring harmonious relations after a conflict has occurred, which often calls for forgiving, forgetting, and moving on.

When your child needs to relate to others in a competitive environment, explain to them that even though they should put forth their best individual effort, they must not pass up opportunities to offer help to others. When your child relates to others in a cooperative environment, suggest that a good team player still does his or her best but in a way that is best for the team as a whole.

87.

Teach Your Child to Respect Adults and to Accept Legitimate Authority

Insist that your child always act respectfully toward adults. This applies not only to adults who have some authority over them, including their teachers, but also to relatives, neighbors, and your friends. Tell your child to show a greater measure of respect to adults than they do to their own friends, even if they happen to dislike or disagree with an adult. Remind your child from time to time that adults, particularly older adults, know far more than children do and have more experience and wisdom than children.

If an adult relative or even a complete stranger happens to correct your child on some occasion and they are largely right in doing so (even if you feel the person is a little out of line), let your child realize that you basically agree with that person. This will indicate to your child that others have the right to judge their actions, will often do so, and possibly rightly so.

Also teach your child that there are adults in government who are elected as the citizens' representatives to pass laws, which must then be obeyed by all members of society. Explain that if citizens don't like certain laws, there are proper ways to try to amend them, but ignoring those laws is not an acceptable option. In fact, violating the law has serious personal and collective consequences. Tell your child to respect those who perform official government duties, because they are acting in accordance with the law to carry out justice and to maintain public safety and order.

88.

Let Your Child Interact Frequently with Adults

Allow your child to develop a fondness for, and basic trust in, other people, and don't seek to shield them from others without good reason. Don't be afraid to let your child become emotionally attached to any of their adult relatives, even those you yourself may not feel particularly close to. More love in your child's heart will surely make them into more loving and caring people. Regular contact with responsible adults will also make your child more mature and responsible. Your child's ability to relate to adults of different backgrounds and personalities will serve them well in life as they'll get to broaden their social skills and go beyond their routine modes of interacting with close friends and family.

Give your child frequent access to their grandparents, aunts and uncles, and other relatives who are generally good influences. Let your child interact with your adult friends and neighbors, and, when appropriate, even with strangers in public (as in a grocery store), without you being overly controlling of those interactions.

Remember that by needlessly limiting your child's access to other adults, not only will your child be deprived as a result, but the adults with whom they might interact will also be deprived of the love and joy your child could bring to their lives.

89.

Teach Your Child Common Sense and Good Judgment

Don't assume that common sense and good judgment will just come to your child over time, but rather make it a point to frequently show them good examples that illustrate these qualities. Explain why you are checking the expiration date on perishable products you buy, why it's more logical to put certain food items in a particular place in the refrigerator, and other such simple examples of daily common sense. Share how you evaluate the pros and cons of various household goods you purchase and how you comparison shop. Share as well examples from your day-to-day life of how common sense and proper planning can help prevent hassles and disappointments in the future.

Have your child articulate periodically why their own actions are consistent with common sense and prudence. Clarify the virtue of prudence as the exercise of good judgment, of heeding good advice rather than being stubborn, and of being aware of likely risks and dangers and taking steps to minimize them. Being prudent also means recognizing that there are people who do not follow the basic principles of morality, and therefore one needs to protect oneself from such people. Tell your child to never go along with anyone they don't know very well. Also tell them that if they leave something of value unattended in a public place, it could very well be stolen by someone with no morals.

Continually develop the faculty of clear thinking in your child by asking them follow-up questions: "And why is this?" "And what would happen then?" Ask your child to think before they act and to realize that every action has consequences. Explain, for instance, that by taking a compromising personal photograph for fun, they may end up embarrassing themselves or others for many decades to come. Tell your child a person always has to consider the consequences of their actions—the more obvious consequences as well as the less obvious ones.

90.

Teach Your Child to Value Their Possessions and to Take Proper Care of Them

A toddler has no understanding of the need to take proper care of physical objects. Banging toys, plucking the leaves off house plants, making a total mess without warning—it's all fair game to a young child. You will quickly realize that preventing your child from wrecking your house is an increasing parental priority.

Though it is best to avoid giving your child easy access to valuable things that could be easily damaged, it is important to develop in them early on a sense that all physical objects have some value. Teach your child that possessions deserve proper care in order to retain their functionality and beauty. Point out how gentle and careful you are when handling household items—when cleaning them or moving them around. Show your child how the smooth surface of a piece of furniture or the shiny display of an electronic device may become blemished if one is careless to scratch or chip them. Ask your child to exercise the greatest care with precious items, and remind them not to damage or lose their own expensive gadgets.

Make the connection for your child between the concept of value and the need to prevent wastefulness. Get them to appreciate that objects and resources are costly and sometimes scarce, and therefore ought to be used judiciously for one's legitimate needs and then reused or recycled if possible. Ask your child to conserve water and electricity, to scrape all the remaining food from a jar, to squeeze a tube of toothpaste for all it's got, and to put perishable food items back in the refrigerator so they won't spoil—all in order to avoid wastefulness. Rest assured, repeated reminders will be required to get all these points across.

91.

Teach Your Child about Money

Perhaps the first lesson you will give your child about money is that it doesn't grow on trees! Beyond that, there are other important lessons you'll want to convey to your child about the role money plays and how adults earn, spend, and save it.

Tell your child that money is used to provide for one's basic needs, and explain what money can and cannot buy. Have your child understand that more money can mean a higher standard of living and greater opportunities in life. Tell them money is obtained through work—the more educated, skilled, resourceful, entrepreneurial, and hard-working a person is, the more money that person can earn. Make it clear, however, that they should try to earn their living in a profession they find personally rewarding and not just financially, and that any money earned must be earned legally and ethically.

Explain that earning money involves a great deal of effort, and spending it—almost none! Therefore, money has to be handled responsibly. A person must create a budget by deciding carefully how much money should be used or saved for which important purpose, and must then keep track of expenses to make sure the budget is adhered to. A desire for impulse purchases needs to be countered with financial self-discipline. If money has to be borrowed temporarily to meet one's needs, it almost always has to be given back with interest.

Tell your child that a portion of the money one earns ought to be set aside not only for expected future expenses, but also for unexpected needs that come up in life from time to time. Money that is saved can be placed in an investment that involves low risk and offers a good return.

Finally, tell your child that the more money one earns, the more generous one needs to be in supporting worthy causes, especially in helping others who are in great need.

92.

Teach Your Child to Be Productive and Not to Procrastinate

Let your child know that feeling lazy is a mood that every person experiences occasionally, but nothing of value gets accomplished if laziness is allowed to linger for long. Tell them it is much more satisfying to be productive and get things done than to procrastinate and waste time. Explain that procrastinators are always worrying about the task they are postponing, and once they finally start working on it, they are stressed over finishing it on time. After procrastinators are done with their task, they realize they could have done a better job if only they had started sooner!

Give your child the understanding that time is highly valuable. Therefore, a person needs to ensure they are spending it well in carrying out their duties, in developing their abilities, in helping others, and in doing the things that will bring them genuine happiness. Tell your child that if they give thought to how they are spending their time, if they are productive, and if they take interest in what they do, their life will unfold to be richly rewarding and fulfilling.

93.

Develop Your Child's Aesthetic Sense, Artistic Talent, and General Creativity

Cultivate your child's sense of aesthetics by pointing out the various aesthetic qualities of objects and places. Show them how shape, size, color, texture, symmetry, and other such attributes are highlighted and arranged, and how these attributes affect the viewer. Also have your child utilize their imagination to create physical objects such as decorations, drawings, and sculptures. See if your child has artistic talent in any other creative field including music, dance, writing, and drama, and help them develop those talents.

Even more important than artistic expression, however, are the broader creative and resourceful aspects of your child's intelligence. These can serve them well in all areas of life by helping them generate better ideas and by stimulating them to find better solutions to problems. Practice brainstorming with your child, and remind them periodically that there may, in fact, be multiple ways to approach and solve any given challenge.

94.

Instill in Your Child a Love of Nature

Nurture in your child a love of nature by spending plenty of time together outdoors, with frequent visits to parks, beaches, lakes, and other nature settings. Express to them how you find the natural world so beautiful, so interesting, and so inspiring.

Tell your child that all animals, which are part of nature, can feel pain, and therefore every person must be careful not to inflict pain on animals. Consider giving your child a pet of their own to take care of, and teach them to look after pets with love and attention in order to ensure the animal's well-being.

Buy your child books and show them movies on various aspects of the natural environment, including the ingenuity and interdependency found in nature. It doesn't matter whether such books or movies are about cats and dogs, insect-eating plants, or how volcanoes work, so long as these books and movies help kindle in your child a love of nature, an appreciation of its intricacy, and an interest in knowing its secrets.

Emphasize to your child that human beings have a duty to keep the environment clean and healthy for all creatures and beautiful and beneficial to all people, including future generations.

95.

Teach Your Child to Be Tolerant

Teach your child that people all over the world are similar in many ways and also different in many ways, with the similarities being greater than the differences. Let your child know about the more apparent differences in appearance, language, culture, and religion, but also in temperament and values. Tell your child it is important to respect and appreciate such diversity, and that one should seek to learn the best of what others have to offer.

Explain that it is wrong to try to force others to think, feel, speak, or act the same way as you do, even when others' opinions, preferences, and behaviors are very different from your own. Ingrain in your child the understanding that every individual has to tolerate all conduct by others, except for harmful conduct that violates the basic rights and freedoms of other people.

Tell your child that every person's home is their private sphere where they can have the widest range of unrestricted personal expression. Outside the home is everyone's shared public sphere where stricter norms of behavior apply, but where each person needs to tolerate the permissible freedom of expression of every other person.

96.

Teach Your Child to Be Considerate and to Develop Empathy and Compassion

Tell your child time and again to be considerate of other people's needs. If Mom is not feeling well and is resting, tell them to keep it quiet because she needs rest in order to feel better, and loud noise will make it difficult for her to get the necessary rest. Ask your child to put themselves in another's shoes and to try to see things from that person's point of view. If their sibling is upset at them, for example, explain to your child what their sibling is perceiving, and then ask your child, "Do you now have a better sense of why your sibling is so upset?" At times, suggest the specific emotions or problems the other person is likely experiencing under the circumstances, thereby gradually causing your child to feel greater empathy for other people.

Teach your child to express interest in the well-being of others. Ask them, for instance, if they remember Grandpa saying he was going in for surgery, and suggest they should ask him how his recovery is coming along the next time they talk to him. Most importantly, teach your child to offer their help not only when they are asked directly, but also when the opportunity presents itself. Tell them to imagine how happy the person will be if someone extends such courtesy and offers assistance.

In short, stress the importance of being considerate, of showing concern for the suffering of others, and of seeking to lighten others' burdens. Tell your child that this is called *compassion*, a noble virtue of feeling connected to others and expressing loving-kindness toward them—people they know and also people they don't know.

97.

Teach Your Child How to Find Inner Peace and Lasting Happiness

Encourage your child to enjoy periods of relative peace and quiet rather than require constant outside stimulation. Tell them it is important to learn how to calm down and relax, and teach them how they can use deep breathing to pacify surging emotions and restore a sense of well-being. Also tell your child they should periodically gather their thoughts, quiet their mind, and reconnect with their "center."

Instill the understanding that desires are potentially unlimited, and that unwise multiplication of desires for material things, sensory pleasures, and superficial thrills leads away from contentment, peace, and happiness, as does coveting what belongs to others.

Teach your child that happiness rests not only on being grateful for what they have and appreciative of what others do for them, but also on having no unfounded expectations from others or from life itself. Convey to your child that happiness comes from inner growth and overcoming, and not from seeking to compete or do battle with anyone or anything outside themselves. Let your child know that happiness flows from fulfilling all of one's duties, especially the duty to contribute to others' happiness.

If you are religiously or spiritually inclined, awaken in your child the awareness that Spirit is ever-present within, without, and among people who relate to one another in virtue and in love, and that living with this awareness is the basis for the deepest and most enduring kind of peace and happiness.

Teach Your Child about Their Obligations to the Community, the Nation, and the World

Tell your child about their future obligation to be of service to others and to give back to the community that helped nurture them. Explain that society is founded on the contributions of all its members, who fulfill various duties and functions that help make everything possible, from the food your child eats, to the gadgets they use, to the roads they travel on. Encourage your child to one day do their part to contribute to the general welfare and the advancement of society.

Help your child realize the great need for being charitable and helping the poor, the sick, and the disabled. Let them know that the more one gives of oneself, the more one receives, making giving truly a joy and a privilege.

Teach your child to love their country and to help preserve all that is good in it. Celebrate national holidays and explain their meaning and significance. Inform your child about the bravery of soldiers and about their noble service and sacrifice.

Tell your child that history stretches far back in time, and that all those who have acted wisely on their desire to do good to others have left the world a better place than the world they came into.

99.

Teach Your Child the Common Skills Adults Need to Know

By the time your child leaves the nest, make sure you have taught them the basic skills independent adults need to have. This includes common practical abilities such as bill paying, cooking, and cleaning. Also practice with your child the essential skill of prioritizing. Explain it as the process of determining what is less or more important, what is less or more urgent, and ranking accordingly the order of what needs to be accomplished.

In their mid-teens, start to introduce your child to various career options and encourage them to explore their career inclinations, if they have any. Keep in mind that your child might not benefit from a liberal arts education as much as they would from a technical-vocational education—or vice versa—so don't dismiss any possibilities. Tell your child that whichever occupation they end up choosing, if they acquire in advance the skills to get along well with other people, if they have a good work ethic, and if they are competent and professional, they will be highly valued by their employers and colleagues.

And last, but not least, give your child some instruction on raising children, so that one day, they too can become wise parents.

100.

Make Frequent Use of Teachable Moments and Convey Life Lessons

In the course of day-to-day life, point out to your child examples that serve to illustrate and reinforce the lessons, skills, and traits you have been trying to convey to them. Whether it is an event you and your child experience directly, an incident told by a relative, or something shown on television, remember that illustrations for valuable lessons can be found all around, and that life is the biggest university of all.

Teach your child that wisdom consists of lessons about life and how best to live it. With more wisdom, one can make better choices. Tell them, for example, that whatever a person puts out in life to others—good or bad—usually ends up coming back to that person in kind, making the choice for good the only wise choice. Remind your child that they have yet to acquire a lot of wisdom, and that gaining wisdom is a lifelong pursuit. Tell them that the insights of wisdom regarding oneself, others, and life as a whole—when applied—result in deeper understanding, greater happiness, and more fulfilling relationships.

Also teach your child that in life there are two ways to learn: the easy way and the hard way. Learning the easy way means following the teachings of wisdom, learning from the mistakes of others, and trying one's best not to repeat one's own mistakes. Learning the hard way means learning only after repeating the same mistakes over and over and suffering the pain and negative consequences again and again. Tell your child to always try to learn the easy way, but whichever way learning occurs, to keep pursuing a life of purpose and meaning; a life consistent with morality and guided by wise principles; a life expressed in honorable action, fulfillment of duty, and service to others; a life of well-rounded personal growth and mutually rewarding relationships; a life of goodness, truth, and beauty; an integral life—a well-lived life.

About the Author

With a lifelong interest in the fields of psychology and practical philosophy, author Dean Michaels has studied the many ancient and modern teachings on human nature and its potential for development. He shares his breadth of knowledge and unique insights through his writings and dedicated personal instruction. Born in Jerusalem, he came to the United States to pursue an education at UCLA (graduating *summa cum laude*) and UC Hastings College of the Law (earning a *Juris Doctor* degree). Dean Michaels' next and most comprehensive work—*The Great Book of Wisdom*—is due to be published in 2014.